# All About Me!

by: Tequila E. Howard, Ed.D

Illustrated by: Laila Lee

**ARPress**
ILLUMINATING IDEAS.
EMPOWERING VOICES

ARPress
45 Dan Road Suite 15
Canton MA 02021

Hotline:  1(888) 821-0229
Fax:       1(508) 545-7580

Ordering Information:
Quantity sales. Special discounts are available on quantity purchases by corporations, associations, and others. For details, contact the publisher at the address above.

Printed in the United States of America.

ISBN-13:  Paperback  979-8-89389-340-3
          eBook       979-8-89389-341-0
          Hardback    979-8-89676-414-4

Library of Congress Control Number: 2024916196

# All About Me!

by: Tequila E. Howard, Ed D

Illustrated by: Laila Lee

# DEDICATION

I dedicate this book to children in all corners of the world. Wishing you blessings in every continent, country, city, village, community, and home. May this book inspire you to become all that you can be.

I am independent!

Who Am I?

I am creative!

# Who Am I?

I am grateful!

# Who Am I?

# I am lovable!

I am a great leader!

I am a strong reader!

Who Am I?

I am family-centered!

Who Am I?

I am effortful!

Who Am I?

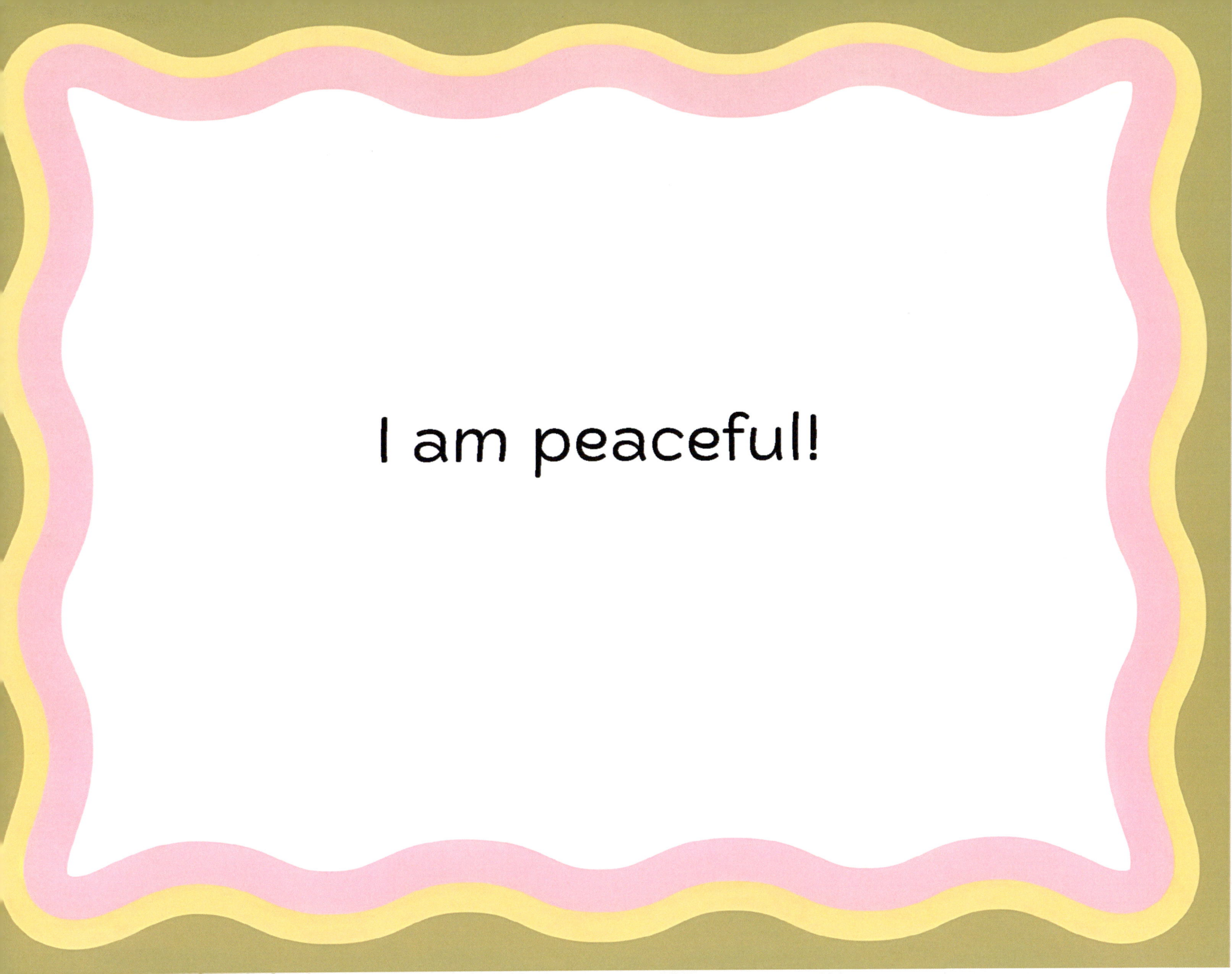

I am peaceful!

Who Am I?

I am friendly!

Who Am I?

I am confident!

# Who Am I?

I am helpful!

Who Am I?

# I am playful!